Dark Is The River

A COLLECTION OF POETRY

BY

Caterina Cimino

SELF-PUBLISHED

2023

For those who seek
their inner glow

Preface

Dear Reader,

Welcome to my poetry anthology, a collection of words and stories inspired by the poets of the past who have captured my imagination and shaped my love for the written word.

From a very young age, I have been drawn to the dark, mysterious, gothic yet wondrous, enchanting and romantic style of poets.

Through the years I have tried to channel that same sense of gloom and magic in my own creative process and Poetry has been the ideal medium to express it, for it has always held a special place in my heart.

I hope that through this anthology, you will find the same wonder and emotion that I have felt while writing it.

Caterina

Synopsis

Across graveyards, forests and ancient halls,
    We wander through the darkest walls,
A thread guides us on our way,
    To delve into the twilight, deep and cold.

We plunge into the River's depths,
    Where obscurity lurks and secrets kept,
We seek a path that we may find,
    To emerge from Shadow, into Light refined.

Poems

Dark Is The River

The Ball

A Ball, it was held, in a grand hall of old,
    With music and laughter, and stories to
      be told.
The guests, they arrived, all dressed in their
      best
    Ready to dance and revel, and put all to
      rest.

But as the night wore on, a strange feeling
      crept,
    A sense of unease, that to all it be kept.
The guests, they grew pale, and their eyes,
      they did freeze,
    As if caught in a spell, or some dark,
      wicked disease.

And then, with a flash, they all vanished
    away,
    Leaving behind only whispers, and a ghostly
    array.
The Ball, it was empty, save for the eerie
    sound
    Of laughter and music, that no longer
    did abound.

And so beware of the ghostly Ball,
    Where the guests, they may seem, but
    in truth, they are all
But spirits and shadows, that dance through
    the night
    A haunting reminder, of a past that took
    flight.

Flower

There is a Flower, fair and pure
    Whose petals are a shade of violet, as
    deep as a bruise.

Some say it is cursed, a symbol of sin and
    decay
    For those who pluck its petals, or even
    gaze upon its beauty
Are doomed to a fate of misery and despair.

Yet I, I cannot resist its allure
    I'm powerless to its magic,
It's a force I cannot ignore.

I hold it in my hand, I feel a surge of excite-
    ment
    A rush of pleasure, a thrill of the forbid-
    den.

As the petals start to wilt and die
    I see the truth in the Flower's curse:
It cannot stay alive.

For as beauty fades, so does my happiness
    Leaving behind an emptiness
The eternal damnation of the Flower.

Necklace

Tears fall like dew,
  A gentle, misty veil.
They flow from heart and soul,
  Like a shattered tale.

At first they seem a burden,
  A yoke that holds us down.
But as they fall and gather,
  They start to take on crown.

For in the end, these tears,
  Become the most precious necklace.
A string of shining pearls,
  That we wear with pride and grace.

For they represent our struggles,
  The agony and woe we've known.
But they also symbolize,
  The resilience and fortitude we've shown.

So let the tears fall,
    And add to this gleaming chain.
For they are not a weakness,
    But a sign of all we've gained.

For through the darkest hours,
    We've learned to stand and endure.
And these tears, like precious pearls,
    Shine bright with all our might.

The Rose

The Rose's thorn is sharp and cruel,
    But without it, the flower is dull.
For beauty and pain are intertwined,
    Like the Rose and its thorn, forever en-
        twined.

Oh Love

Oh Love, thou art a fickle fiend
    Thy fire doth burn, with a vicious gleam
Thy touch doth scorch, with a fiery kiss
    Leaving me, to writhe, in thy abyss.

Thou art a poison, that doth course through
      my veins
    Thy sweetness doth mask, thy venomous
    pains
Thy embrace doth smother, with a deadly
      hold
    Leaving me, to suffocate, in thy cold.

Thou art a curse, that doth haunt my dreams

    Thy whispers doth echo, with sinister
    schemes
Thy gaze doth pierce, with a malevolent
    stare
    Leaving me, to tremble, in thy snare.

But yet, I crave thee, with a hunger fierce
I long for thee, even in my worst fears
For in thy Enigma, I find a glimmer of hope
That one day, I'll break free from thy
yoke.

As Above, So Below

As Above, so Below,
    Mirrored reflections,
Earth and Sky,
    In a tapestry of Time.

The Mirror

In the darkest corner of the room,
　　There sits a mirror, old and grim
Its frame is carved from ancient wood
　　And its surface is clouded and dim.

I approach it with trepidation
　　For I know not what secrets it holds
As I gaze into its depths, I see
　　My own reflection, twisted and cold.

The face that stares back at me
　　Is not my own, but a stranger's guise
Its eyes are hollow and empty
　　And its lips twist into a sinister smile.

I feel a chill run down my spine
　　As I wonder who, or what, I see
Is this the reflection of my soul
　　Or the spirit of some entity?

I turn to leave, but the mirror calls to me
    Its voice a whisper in my ear
It beckons me to stay
    And to confront my greatest fear.

I hesitate

Torn between flight or sight
    The mirror's call, a siren's plight.

Mysteries that Never Die

Nature, in all her wild and wondrous guise,
　　With beauty that astounds, and myster-
　　　ies that never die.
She speaks to us, in her own silent way
　　Of secrets kept, and tales yet to say.

Her winds, they howl, and her branches,
　　they creak
　　As she whispers her stories, and chroni-
　　　cles that she keeps.
Her skies, they turn, from blue to grey
　　As she tells her legends, in her own mys-
　　　terious way.

Her mountains, they rise, and her valleys,
　　they fall
　　As she reveals her secrets, to one and to
　　　all.
Her oceans, they rage, and her rivers, they
　　flow
　　As she shares her insights, with a voice
　　　that's aglow.

Nature, in all her wild and wondrous guise
With beauty that astounds, and myster-
ies that never die.

The King of Elves

Though wrinkles line the hand that holds,
    the knife that cuts the fruit of love,
the gesture speaks a truth untold,
    that age can nurture, from above.

Tree of Life

In the dappled woods, a Tree doth stand,
    Whose branches reach to Heaven's blue
        span.
Its leaves a rustling, whispered song,
    A gnarled masterpiece its bough long.

Some say the old gods did plant this Tree,
    Its roots run deep, reaching down to the
        very heart of the Earth, you see.
Its leaves hold power, both pure and true,
    To heal and grant eternal life anew.

But be warned, traveler of the night,
    To plunder this Tree is not right.
For it is sacred, a guardian of the Land
    And it will not suffer abuse at any man's
        hand.

If your heart is candid, a blessing you may
    receive
      But if not, turn and flee, or you'll be
      deceived.
For the secrets of the Tree are only meant
    for those
      Who believe.

Maddening

The sink, it leaked, a steady drip,
    A sound that echoed through the house,
      a nagging quip.
It seemed a minor nuisance at first glance,
    But as the days went on, it grew in cir-
      cumstance.

The water pooled and seeped below,
    An ever-growing puddle that began to
      grow.
The wood around it rotted and decayed:
    A sight that filled me with dismay.

I tried to fix it, I tried with all my might
    But no matter what I did, the leak dripped
      all night.
I called a plumber, I begged and pleaded
    But still the leak, it never receded.

It seemed to mock me, this leaky sink,
 A constant reminder of my inability to
  think.

And so I lived with it, day after day
 This leaky sink that seemed to have its
  way.
A constant presence, a nagging sound
 A reminder of my own shortcomings, for-
  ever bound.

I could bare it no more,
 I tore it out, and through the door
I cast it, a broken, leaking thing
 A relief to be rid of it, my heart did sing.

The leak was gone, the sound no more
 Yet the echo of that sink, it lingers on
A haunting rhyme,
 A never ending strain
Of the things that drive us

   Insane.

Hazelnut

Nature's tender Gem,
    Soft and sweet.
Precious Hazelnut,
    Fairies' Golden Gift.

Open Wound

My heart is an open wound,
    An emptiness, that cannot be filled
It is a scar, that marks my chest
    And reminds me, every day, of my pain.

My heart is an extinguished flame
    An ember, that cannot be reignited
It is ash, that dissolves in the wind
    And leaves me, alone and without
        shelter.

My heart is a sharp blade
    A sword, that pierces my chest
It is a blade, that cannot be put away
    And leaves me, on the ground,
        defenseless.

My heart is a dark labyrinth
    A maze, that cannot be explored
Without an escape
    And leaves me deplored.

Restless Seas

Like the restless Seas,
    The Mind is always in motion,
Surging and churning with emotion.

The Lamb

In the heart of a gloomy moor,
    Where the winds howl and the shadows
        loom,
There roams a lamb, all alone,
    In this land of impending doom.

His fleece is white as driven snow,
    But it's stained with mud and grime,
For he's been wandering these forsaken
    lands for an eternity of time.

He bleats and cries, a pitiful sound,
    But no one hears his mournful call,
He's lost and lonely, far from home,
    Trapped in this dreary hall.

The moon shines bright, a ghostly light,
    But it offers no comfort or reprieve,
The lamb shivers and shakes,
    As he tries to find a way to leave.

But the moors are vast and wild,
 And the lamb is small and weak,
He knows he'll never find his way,
 To the pastures where the grass is sweet.

So he lays down in the cold, hard earth,
 And closes his eyes, resigned to fate,
A sacrifice to the twisted moors,
 A lamb to the eerie state.

Coffers of Tears

A Thousand coffers of tears,
    The price
Bargained
    For the wind
To blow me away

The Tarot's Voice

The tarot reader, cloaked in shadow,
    Her cards spread out before her throne,
Mysterious symbols and secrets,
    Laid bare for all to be known.

She beckons me with bony hand,
    Her eyes fixed on my face,
I approach with beating heart,
    Desperate to know my destined place.

She shuffles the deck with practiced grace,
    Then lays the cards in a noble row,
Each one a sign of what is to come,
    A glimpse of what the future doth hold.

The Tower, the Hanged man, the Hermit,
    Each card holds its own weight,
The tarot reader reads them all,
    With a voice both soft and great.

She tells me of love and loss,
　　Of sorrow and of joy,
She speaks of things that I have known,
　　And things that I'll soon employ.

I leave the tarot reader's side,
　　Feeling both elated and small,
I've glimpsed the path that lies ahead,
　　But it's up to me to walk it all.

The Tower

Lightning strikes the Tower,
    Crumbling, falling to the ground
Turmoil is birthed.

The Hanged Man

Odin, suspended sage, the Hanged Man,
    both hanging in their quests,
seeking wisdom's fruit.

The Hermit

Silent meditation,
    Enlightenment
Inner Truth's bright glow.

Skull

Un-Venerable skull,
    Hollow shell,
Of Seas bountiful,
    Ancient tale it has to tell.

Etched in his suture,
    An engraving of my future.
Truth that cannot fail,
    Holy, Un-holy grail.

Chrysanthemum

Most delicate cupbearer,
　　To sip from its petals
To stain lips
　　Is to drink
Not the poison of death
　　But blood
Sweetest wine
　　Of life

Cypresses

In the old cemetery, where the dead do lay,
    The dawn sky is painted by the Lord's
       own hand,
With cypress trees as His paintbrushes
    grand, their branches reaching for the
       heavenly land.

The morning light doth filter through
    Their leaves of dark and somber hue,
Creating shadows on the ground,
    A peaceful and serene view.

The cypress stand tall and proud,
    Their branches strong and true,
Guiding us through the graves
    To a place of solace and peace anew.

The Virgin

The virgin alone, her white dress torn,
    By the thorns and brambles of the wild,
Her eyes fixed on the ghost that haunts the
      glade,
    Whose blood-stained hands reach out in
      desperate need.

The cobwebs hang like silver threads,
    Entwining the branches and the trunks
      of the wood,
Trapping the ghost in their sticky embrace,
    As she approaches with a cold, steady
      tread.

The ghostly figure pleads for mercy,
    But the virgin's heart is hard and
      unyielding,
For she knows the power of the blood that
      stains the earth,
    And the secrets hidden in the heart of
      the Forest.

Eternity

Flowers constantly die,
　　Even in Spring,
Before blossoming.
　　But the leaves
Persist over time,
　　As a precious legacy
Of the spirit of the Bud.

Windows

There once was a room, dark and drear,
  Where portraits hung, their eyes so clear
In the night, they seemed to glow
  Their gazes fixed, as if they'd know.

But in the light of morning's hue,
  The truth was revealed, as clear as dew:
The portraits were just windows,
      plain to see
  No eyes, no soul, just empty, clear glass
  staring back at me.

The room, once filled with shadows and fear,
  Now just a simple space, without any
      mystery or leer.
Yet the query lingers, deep inside:
  Were those eyes real, did they ever sub-
      side?

Soul

What is Soul searching for

My veins and my blood
 Must be
Pumping, flowing
 Through the roots

Keep it safe
 Keep it still
As when it runs
 I'm up above
The crown
 Of the ancient Tree

Age and Brother

Love lost in the Dark River,
    Age and brother, forever gone
Shivers crawl, distant quiver.

In this spectral realm
    I am but a ghost,
Forever doomed to wander
    Through the shadows of my past.

The Dark River flows on,
    Unyielding,
Uncaring,
    Unfolding.

Age and brother, love lost,
    Shadows sowed, reaped frost.

The Cathedral

The Forest,
 An ancient cathedral,
A place of worship and of awe,
 Where time stands still and nature
  reigns, a sanctuary, a holy law.

The trees, they are the pillars,
 The leaves, the stained glass on high,
The moss, the carpet beneath our feet,
 The branches, the ceiling reaching to the
  sky.

The wind, it sings the hymns,
 The birds, they chirp the choir,
The streams, they flow with holy water,
 The pine, a sacred spire.

We enter with hushed reverence,
 Our footsteps soft and light,
For in this ancient cathedral,
 We feel the presence of the divine.

The Forest, a sacred place,
　　A sanctuary from the world,
We let our spirits be unfurled.

Reverie

There's a sound that echoes through the
     night,
  A whisper soft and strange and bright.
It calls to me, and I obey:
  Follow me, toward a secret bay.

I wander through the halls and rooms
  My footsteps echoing in the gloom
I search for the source of the eerie noise
  That grows louder, a near voice.

I turn a corner, and there it is
  A glowing orb, that floats and glistens
It pulsates with energy and light
  As the sound reaches a frenzied height.

I grasp to touch the orb, to feel its heat
  But as my fingers near, it disappears
Disintegrating into a shower of sparks
  Leaving me in the darkness, and in the
     dark.

Was it a dream, a hallucination
    Or something more, a revelation?

That sound,
    The memory,
Will stay with me forever,
    A mystery,
That haunts my thoughts:
    My Reverie.

Our Lady of The Woods

I stand before the Lady of the Woods,
    Watching her limbs stretch to the sky,
The wind murmuring through her silver locks
      so high
    As I drink the sap that flows within her
      veins
I savor the essence of the earth,
    The very breath of the divine,
My senses heightened,
    As I've tasted the Birch,

The elixir of Life.

The Language of Flowers

The floral tongue, a cryptic lexicon,
    A silent tongue of petals bright,
That speaks of love and pure delight.

Still flowers may also bear despair,
    A thistle for misanthropy, a sneer,
A dandelion for a broken heart,
    A wilted rose, a love departs.

Yet even in sorrow, flowers bring,
    A sense of beauty, a comforting fling
We must cherish the language of flowers,
    A means of expressing our deepest pow-
        ers.

The Ħeart of a Pirate

In the depths of the abyss, where darkness
 reigns supreme,
  Lurk the oldest and most terrifying crea-
  tures unseen.
But perhaps you know not of the darkest
 secret of all,
  A secret hidden deep beneath the waves
  and the squall.

One day, sailing through a stormy sea, you'll
 hear a sound,
  A deafening noise, a deep rumble, an op-
  pressive bound.
The waves will take control, and the water
 will close in,
  Leaving you with nothing but silence amid
  the din.

But fear not, for the will of the sea is un-
predictable and fickle,
Calm waters cannot last, and soon the
waves will start to prickle.
The sea comes alive again, a crumpled blue
mantle,
In the chaos of turmoil, with a persis-
tent, piercing rattle.

The sailors don't know where it comes from,
but they know what it means,
A final test, a choice between life and
death, or so it seems.
With each dull blow, a wave breaks, and a
sailor's heart stops beating,
But as the wave emerges, it starts again,
now with vigor, a pirate's greeting.

So if you hear that sound, that ominous,
ominous noise,
Don't be afraid, for it's only the test, the
ultimate choice.
Will you let yourself die, or will you embrace
life's thrill?
The choice is yours, but remember, the
sea's will is free to spill.

Time

Time passes by like waves on the shore,
    Ebb and flow, forevermore.
It rustles like the leaves on a tree,
    Softly whispering, constantly.
It cascades like a waterfall so grand,
    Rushing forward, out of hand.
It lingers like a lover's kiss,
    Soft and sweet, in endless bliss.
It dances like the wind in the sky,
    Gentle and free, never to die.

Cloak

A foggy cloak enshrouds the earth
 A thick, oppressive mist that blots out
  all mirth.
Only the faintest glimmers break through
  the gloom,
 Like dying stars in a never-ending tomb.
The world is buried in obscurity,
 As the fog descends and engulfs every-
  thing.
The town slips away,
 Leaving only the weakest flickers of light
  astray.
They lead us through the abyss,
 Guiding us home across the mist's icy
  kiss.
But as we near the safety of the light,
 The sparks go out, leaving us to the night.

Monarch

Gentle monarch roams,
    Graceful steps through Forest wild,
Deer reigns supreme.

The Dance of the Druids

Forever to Soar,
　　With the old gods, their spirits nigh.
Weathered stones, a sacred ring.

A dance of the Druids, blissful and wild
　　Elements called, voices sing
Hearts beguiled.

Power reborn, circle's might
　　Honor the old, dance through the night
Ancient lore, fire burns right.

Hearts clear,
　　Spin with pure Light.

Mountain

Mountain stands before me
    beacon of raw power
rugged, rocky slopes
    natural, majestic tower.

Mountain, your beauty lies
    In your untamed grace.
A deer,
    I am in love
With your undressed face

The Lonely Wolf

Through the trees,
    Haunting wail,
Echoes through the night,
    A gale.

Cry full of sorrow and despair
    Piercing the air,
Mournful flair.

Wind howls,
    Shadows play tricks,
The wolf's voice reaches its peak.

He is but
    A Man

Lost in the forest,
    Pitiful sound,
Doomed to wander:
    Forever bound.

Nectar

What we hold within our grasp,
    A droplet of nectar,
Extracted from the bloom that blooms
    In the darkest hours of the moor.

The ebon flower that blossoms
    When the Moon is at its height,
He shies away from its beguiling charms,
    But I suspect you might
Not.

For within its depths, one can discern
    The fate of the world,
And the light is where all desire to be,
    Everyone
Everyone except me.

Wanderer

Intoxication of stillness beckons me,
    Its warmth envelops, fear it sets free.
Enraptured by its glowing embrace,
    A sense of peace, of letting go takes its
        place.

The fire within burns bright,
    Flames of life reach for the sky.
For in this stillness, this rapture divine,
    I am alive, I am alive

Life and Death

Yet Love, it never truly fades,
    It lingers on, a constant thread
Love so deep, it breaks the veil
    Of life and death, of joy and wail

It dwells within the shadows of the heart
    A silent whisper, a constant art
Love so strong, it braves the night
    Of life and death, of wrong and right

It whispers through the ages past
    A timeless melody, Love that lasts
Love so true, it breaks the chains
    Of life and death, of joy and pains

It lives within the hearts of those
    Who bear the weight, who brave the woes

Love so pure, it conquers all
    Of life and death, of rise and fall

White Buffalo

Crossing paths,
    Lustrous ivory
Of worshipful tears
    Black piercing opals

        Bow

At your sight
At your might,
    White Buffalo,

        I Bow

The Moon

Cloud-veiled bride Moon,
    Sight to behold,
As she stands on the altar,
    Enshrouded in gold.

Her handmaids,
    The Stars,
Gently hold her train:
    Celestial scene,
As the cloud-veiled bride Moon,
    Is wed to the sky's gleam.

Falls the gaze,
    Wonder and delight,
For the cloud-veiled bride Moon,
    Is wed to the Night.

Dark Is The River

Dark River's nourishing waters
    Embrace me
For I willingly sink

Emerged renewed
    Spirit soaring high
By the grace within
    My Soul does rise